WHAT IS EMPATHY?

A BULLYING STORYBOOK FOR KIDS

Written by
AMANDA MORIN

Illustrations by
JOHN JOSEPH

ROCKRIDGE
PRESS

WHAT IS EMPATHY?

A BULLYING STORYBOOK FOR KIDS

Written by
AMANDA MORIN

Illustrations by
JOHN JOSEPH

ROCKRIDGE
PRESS

DEAR PARENTS AND CAREGIVERS,

We want what's best for our children. We want to make sure they're safe, compassionate, and able to stand up for themselves. Many parents worry about their kids being bullied, especially at school. This type of mistreatment is a valid concern.

Bullying is a widespread problem. Nearly one in three students in the United States say they've been bullied at school. But not all kids engage in bullying behavior directly. Some kids assist in the bullying, join in with bullying occasionally, or provide an audience for other kids who bully, especially when it comes to the most common types of bullying—verbal and social.

Verbal and social bullying typically involves children working together to exclude or hurt other kids. This type of bullying is shown in this book.

The purpose of this book is to help prevent kids from bullying by teaching them to approach the world with a more empathetic lens. This book was written to show your child the power of understanding another person's point of view. One story is told two ways—first through Sofia's eyes, then through Ava's. The story is written this way to help your child experience empathy while they learn about the concept.

Before you read the book, talk to your child about what they know about bullying. Ask them if they've seen bullying happen at school and what was done about it. Then, as you read this book, ask your child to:

- Point out bullying behavior in the book.
- Discuss how they would have handled the situation.
- Brainstorm ways that bullying can be addressed.

Let your child know that being and feeling safe is important and that they can always tell a trusted adult about bullying. Safety is more important than worrying about being a tattletale.

This book also introduces the idea that empathy is about being curious and kind at the same time. As you read the story together, you can reinforce this idea for your child. Here are some concepts and questions to encourage thoughtful discussions:

- **People feel like you're curious about them when you notice how they'd like to be treated and you treat them that way.** *Can you point out a time when one of the characters in the book treated another character how they wanted to be treated?*

- **Asking open-ended questions is both curious and kind.** Open-ended questions are questions that you don't already know the answer to. These kinds of questions don't assume you know how someone is feeling or know what's on their mind. *Can you find an example of when an adult asked an open-ended question in this book?*

- **Sometimes people feel blamed when they hear "you" sentences,** such as "You hurt my feelings." But when that sentence is turned into an "I" sentence, like "I feel hurt when you ignore me," people feel better. *When did you hear "you" sentences in this book? When did you hear "I" sentences? What happened in each situation?*

The good news about bullying is that studies have shown that adults have the power to stop it. When adults talk to kids about bullying, encourage kids to talk to *them* about bullying, and model compassion, respect, and empathy, they help prevent bullying.

Bullying is complicated and not as simple as one child picking on or harming another. Some kids who engage in bullying have trouble connecting with other people's feelings.

Empathy is one way of connecting. It is a person's ability to see another person's point of view, to try to understand another person's feelings, and to let another person know that they are understood. Keep in mind that understanding a person is not the same as agreeing with them!

Empathy alone will not end bullying, nor should we ask kids to excuse bullying behavior because they have empathy for the child who is bullying them. But teaching kids to be compassionate *can* be one preventive measure against bullying.

When we understand how we are more alike than different, when we pause to think about a different perspective before acting, and when we respond from a place of curiosity and kindness, we are less likely to view *different* as *less* and more likely to think before acting in hurtful ways.

For more information and statistics, visit **www.stopbullying.gov**.

HELLO, READERS!

Have you ever heard two people tell the same story? That's what happens in this book. One story is told two ways—first through Sofia's eyes, then through Ava's. And that story is about bullying.

The story is also about best friends and the power of something called empathy. Empathy is a way of being curious and kind at the same time. Having empathy is like being a detective. When you have empathy, you are being curious, which means you're paying attention to how other kids act. Having empathy means you're asking other kids questions to figure out how they feel. And, in order to be a good detective, you need to ask those questions kindly. You need to think about how being kind might change how someone else acts.

As you read this book, pay attention to how Sofia and Ava learn to understand each other better. What happens when they are curious and kind?

When people act like bullies, they may hurt your feelings. They might make you feel bad about yourself. They may even hurt your body. Being curious and kind can help prevent bullying. But it's never okay for someone to act like a bully. Being kind to someone does not mean you should let them bully you. If you're being bullied or see someone else being bullied, always tell an adult you trust so they can help you.

Part One: Sofia's Story

Sofia had been waiting for the first day of school.
It meant she could see Ava again!

Sofia and Ava were best friends.
They both loved bubble gum ice cream.
They both snort-laughed when their giggling
got out of control. Ava was the only person Sofia
told her biggest secrets to.

Ava and Sofia even used to live next door to each other.
But last spring, Sofia's family had to move across town.

Sofia's mom worked all day and didn't have a car. It was too far for
Sofia to bike to Ava's house by herself, so she hadn't seen Ava all summer!

Sofia knew Ava would save her a seat on the bus. They always sat together.

But when Sofia got on the bus, she saw Ava sitting with a girl she didn't know.

Sofia stopped at Ava's seat and smiled.

"I'm so happy to see you. Move over!" Sofia said.

The new girl frowned. "I sit here. Ava is *my* friend."

Sofia waited for Ava to move over, but she didn't.

Ava just looked at Sofia, raised her eyebrows, and shrugged.

Sofia saw her friend Liam in another seat, watching.

She hoped he didn't notice she was crying.

"Come sit with me," Liam called.
"You got glasses? They're so cool!"

"Yeah," Sofia replied. "I can see so much better."
She sniffled and wiped her face on her sleeve.
"Who was that girl? Why was she so mean? And
why didn't Ava tell her that I'm her best friend?"
Sofia asked.

"She must be new," Liam said.
"I'm sure Ava will stick up for you next time."

But as the days went by, Ava did not stick up for Sofia.

Ava and her new friend Madison even picked on her.

At lunch, they told Sofia, "You can't sit here. Too bad!"

At recess, they told Sofia, "Sorry, this game is full. You can't play."

But Sofia knew this wasn't true. She saw Madison and Ava
sitting with other kids at lunch and playing with them at recess.

Sofia missed her best friend and was sad that she had moved.
She couldn't just walk over to Ava's house for a sleepover.
They didn't get to eat ice cream together after school.

Now. Ava didn't even giggle with her at school. Sofia was lonely.

Why didn't Ava like her anymore?

The worst day came three weeks later.

"Did you see Sofia's shirt?" Madison asked kids at lunch.
"Ava gave it to her because her mom can't afford to buy new clothes.
Sofia only wears hand-me-downs."

Sofia's face turned red. Only Ava knew that.
How could Ava tell her biggest secret?

"You should tell the teacher," Liam said.

Sofia didn't want to be a tattletale. She didn't know what to do.

She was in a pickle. That's what her mom called any problem that didn't have an easy answer. Sofia always remembered her mom's saying because she didn't like pickles. She didn't like *being* in a pickle either.

But if Mom knew about being in pickles, maybe she knew how to get out of pickles, too.

"Mom, I'm in a pickle," she told her mom that night.

"What kind of pickle?" Mom asked.

Sofia told Mom everything. She told her that thanks to Madison, everybody in class knew Sofia's biggest secret.

Sofia whispered, "I think Madison is a bully. And I think Ava might be a bully now, too."

Mom hugged Sofia tight. "That's a big pickle," she said.
"I bet you feel sad and lonely. It does sound like they are acting like bullies."

"Acting like bullies? They *are* bullies." Sofia exclaimed.

"How people act is different from who they are." Mom said.
"I think Ava might be angry because we moved away.
 Maybe that's why she's bullying you.
 We should try to have some empathy for Ava."

Sofia didn't know what empathy was.

"It's when you're able to see things through someone else's eyes."
Mom explained. "I know that's hard to do when you're feeling hurt.
But maybe you can try."

As she fell asleep, Sofia wondered about empathy. Was it a superpower? *Could* she have it? How could she make Ava see through *her* eyes?

The next day at recess, Sofia handed Ava her glasses.

"Put these on and look at Madison," Sofia demanded.

Ava shook her head.

Sofia wanted Ava to have empathy. She stamped her foot.

"Put them on!" Sofia shouted. "I want you to see through my eyes."

"Mrs. Hall," Madison called. "Sofia is bullying Ava. She's yelling and trying to make her do something she doesn't want to do."

Mrs. Hall took Sofia aside. "You and Ava are having a hard time this year. Why don't you tell me what's going on?"

"I just wanted Ava to have empathy." Sofia said.

"What do your glasses have to do with empathy?" Mrs. Hall asked.

Sofia explained that she wanted Ava to see things through her eyes.

Mrs. Hall smiled. "I understand," she said. "That's very wise of you, Sofia. But empathy doesn't mean *really* seeing through someone else's eyes. It means knowing what it's like to be in their shoes."

Sofia told Mrs. Hall how she and Ava got matching sneakers when they were best friends. "Ava is still wearing them, Mrs. Hall. Do you think Ava's sneakers can give her empathy?"

Mrs. Hall smiled again. "I think it's a good sign that Ava still wears them. But that's not exactly what I meant. It's just a saying," she told Sofia. "Being in someone else's shoes means being curious about what it feels like to be them and why they act the way they do. You can't make people feel empathy. You can only be kind and hope they learn from you."

Back in class, Sofia stopped at Ava's seat. "I'm sorry about today," Sofia said.

Madison rolled her eyes.

"It's okay, Sofia," Ava said.

Madison was angry. "Why did you tell her it's okay?
You're *my* friend!" she huffed.

This confused Sofia. Why did Madison think
Ava should have only one friend?

On the bus the next day, Ava was sitting alone.
Madison was giggling with a girl Sofia didn't know.

Sofia watched Ava's eyes fill with tears. She remembered what Mrs. Hall said about being curious. She thought about how sad she was feeling without Ava as her friend. She wondered if that's how Ava felt now.

Sofia could understand these feelings through Ava's eyes.
She knew what it felt like to be in Ava's shoes.

Sofia was feeling empathy!

Sofia noticed that Madison and her new friend had started picking on Ava.

They didn't make room for Ava at lunch or play with her at recess.

Sofia was still mad, and her feelings were still hurt. But she remembered what Mom said about trying to have empathy anyway.

"Ava, come sit with us," Sofia called. "Then we can all swing together at recess."

At the end of the week, Ava said, "I'm sorry I was mean, Sofia. I was sad when you moved. Madison moved in next door. She said she'd be my new friend."

Sofia knew how scary it was to move to a new house.
She also knew how sad she'd been that Ava had a new friend.

She wondered if that's how Madison felt, too.

Sofia was thinking about why Madison was acting the way she did.

She was feeling empathy again.

It was something she could feel for everybody!

"Let's stand up to Madison together. But let's do it in a kind way," Sofia said.
Then she told Ava what she knew about empathy.

When Sofia got on the bus the next day, she stopped at Madison's seat and said hello.

Madison frowned. "Why are you talking to me?"

"Because she's a kind friend," said Ava.

Madison glared at Ava. "She's not my friend, and neither are you."

"I am your friend," said Ava. "I'm Sofia's friend, too. I should have told you that a long time ago. We can all be friends."

QUESTIONS TO CONSIDER

The first story was told through Sofia's perspective, or point of view. The next, the story will be told through Ava's point of view. As you read the second story, think about these questions:

1. How are the stories alike? How are they different?

2. Are there parts of the story that are the same through both points of view?

3. Do you feel differently about any of the characters after reading both stories?

4. Do you think it was important to know both points of view?

5. How did empathy play a role in both stories?

BONUS QUESTIONS

1. How do you think the story would be told through Madison's point of view?

2. Can you tell or write Madison's version of the story?

3. Is there another character whose point of view you'd like to hear?

Part Two: Ava's Story

It was the first day of school. Ava was nervous.
She hadn't seen her best friend Sofia since Sofia's family moved across town.

That was a whole summer's worth of bubble gum ice cream that Ava had
to eat without Sofia!

Ava didn't know what would happen when she saw Sofia.
She wasn't sure they were best friends anymore.

They used to always sit together on the bus.
Ava knew Sofia would expect her to save a seat.

But Ava hadn't saved Sofia a seat.

She was sitting with her new friend,
Madison, who had moved into Sofia's
old house. Ava hoped they could all
be friends.

When Sofia got on the bus, she stopped at Ava's seat.
"I'm so happy to see you," she said, smiling. "Move over!"

But before Ava could make room, Madison spoke up.

"I sit here. Ava is *my* friend."

Sofia sat with her friend Liam, and Ava turned to Madison.

"I think you made Sofia cry," Ava said. "I didn't even get to tell her I like her new glasses."

Madison shrugged. "You're my friend now. We spent all summer playing together. If Sofia was *really* your friend, she would have at least come to visit."

Ava thought over what Madison said. Sofia's mom didn't have a lot of money or a car. Sofia would have had to ride her bike to Ava's house. But she couldn't ride that far by herself and her mom worked all day.

Ava hadn't told Madison any of these things.

But maybe Madison was right. Maybe Sofia *should* have found a way to come visit over the summer.

As the days went by, Ava started to feel angry.
After all, Sofia *had* moved away and never visited!

So, Ava didn't stick up for Sofia when Madison picked on her.

At lunch, Madison told Sofia, "You can't sit here. Too bad!"

At recess, Madison said their game was full.
Ava didn't speak up, even though Sofia looked hurt.

But Ava saw Sofia sit with Liam at lunch and play with him at recess.

It seemed to Ava that Sofia had made a new friend. Maybe Sofia *didn't* miss her best friend. That hurt Ava's feelings.

Madison told her it didn't matter.

"I'll be your best friend," she told Ava.
"When I moved here, I had no friends.
 Now I have you. I don't need another friend.
 You don't either."

Then came the worst day.

Sofia came to school wearing a shirt that Ava loved.

"Isn't that shirt cool?" Ava asked Madison.
"I gave it to Sofia when I outgrew it."

"Why?" Madison asked.

"Well, her mom doesn't have a lot of money.
Sofia wears hand-me-downs."

Ava didn't mean to tell Sofia's secret. It just happened.

"*Eww . . .* I wouldn't wear other people's old clothes." Madison said rudely.
She told all the other kids that Sofia couldn't afford new clothes.

Ava knew that Madison wasn't just being mean anymore.
She was bullying Sofia.

But Ava didn't think she could stand up to Madison.
She didn't want Madison to bully her, too.

If Madison bullied her, Ava wouldn't have
any friends left.

She was in what Sofia's mom called a pickle.

"Momma, I think I'm in a pickle,"
Ava said at bedtime.

"What's going on?" Momma asked.

Ava burst into tears.
She told Momma everything.

She told her that she hadn't been sticking up for Sofia.

Then she told Momma what Madison said about only needing one friend.

"I'm angry at Sofia for moving, but I've been mean," said Ava.
"If I were her, I'd be so sad."

Momma thought for a minute. "I'm not happy with how you've acted," she said. "But I'm glad you have some empathy for Sofia."

Ava didn't know what empathy was.

"It's when you're able to understand how someone else might feel," explained Momma.

Ava wondered about empathy. Did Sofia know about it? Could Sofia have empathy for *her*?

The next day at recess. Ava was feeling grumpy again.

She saw Sofia and Liam talking to each other.
They looked like they were having fun.

Ava wanted someone to talk to. She wasn't having any fun.

She didn't think it was fair that Sofia was having fun without her.

When the class lined up to go inside, Sofia stood next to Ava.

Maybe Sofia wanted to be friends again!
Ava decided to tell Sofia she missed her.
But before Ava could tell her, Sofia pushed her glasses into Ava's face.

"Put these on and look at Madison," Sofia demanded.

Ava was confused. She shook her head.

Sofia stamped her foot. "Put them on!" she said, raising her voice.
"I want you to see through my eyes."

"Mrs. Hall," Madison called. "Sofia is bullying Ava.
She's yelling and trying to make her do something she doesn't want to do."

Mrs. Hall took Sofia aside to talk to her.
It looked like Sofia was trying not to cry.

"Why did you say that?" Ava asked Madison. "She wasn't bullying me.
If anyone is a bully, it's *you*. You've been mean to Sofia since
the very first day of school."

Now it looked like Madison was trying not to cry.
"I'm not a bully," she said.
"I was just making sure you'd keep being my friend.
Besides, you were mean, too."

Ava didn't know what to say. Madison was right.
They had both been mean.

But Madison was also wrong.
Why did she think Ava would stop being her friend?

Back in class, Sofia stopped at Ava's seat.
"I'm sorry about today," she said.

Ava smiled. "It's okay, Sofia."

Madison was still angry.

"Why did you tell her it's OK? You're *my* friend!" Madison huffed.
"If you're going to be Sofia's friend, you can't be mine anymore."

At lunch, Madison told Ava,
"You can't sit here. Too bad!"

At recess, Madison said,
"Sorry, this game is full. You can't play."

Ava took a deep breath. "I'm sorry I was mean, Sofia," she said.
"I was sad when you moved. Madison moved in next door.
She said she'd be my new friend. But why are you being so kind to me?"

"I know what it's like to be in your shoes. I was sad when you stopped being my friend." Sofia said. "I can even see through Madison's eyes. It's scary to move and not know anybody in the neighborhood. I wonder if that's how Madison feels. Maybe that's why she's acting this way."

Ava remembered what Momma said about being able to understand how someone else might feel. "Do you know about empathy, too?" she asked.

Sofia laughed. "Yes! At first, I thought it was a superpower."

Then Sofia thought for a moment and said, "Let's stand up to Madison together. But let's do it in a kind way."

Ava watched as Sofia got on the bus the next day.
Sofia stopped at Madison's seat and said hello.

Madison frowned. "Why are you talking to me?"

"Because she's a kind friend," said Ava.

Madison glared at Ava. "She's not my friend, and neither are you."

"I am your friend," said Ava.
"I'm Sofia's friend, too.
I should have told you that a long time ago.
We can all be friends."

Maybe the three girls wouldn't be *best* friends. But they were off to a good start.

Ava was pretty sure Sofia was right. Empathy was a superpower after all.

AMANDA MORIN is a former classroom teacher and early intervention specialist. She's an education writer and special education advocate, and she serves as an in-house adviser for Understood.org, where she teaches about using empathy as a tool to understand difference and embrace inclusion. Morin is the author of *The Everything Parent's Guide to Special Education*, *The Everything Kids' Learning Activities Book*, and *On-the-Go Fun for Kids!* She lives in coastal Maine with her family.

JOHN JOSEPH is an award-winning *New York Times* best-selling illustrator of more than a dozen books for children. When he is not creating books, he spends his days creating art with over 500 elementary school students as a full-time visual arts teacher. After school, he facilitates two student groups that focus on bully prevention, asset building, and community outreach. He lives in Colorado with his wife and two young boys.

Interior and Cover Designer: Angela Navarra
Art Producer: Meg Baggott
Editor: Barbara J. Isenberg
Production Manager: Martin Worthington
Production Editor: Melissa Edeburn

Illustration © 2020 John Joseph
Author photo courtesy of Jacob Lewis Media

ISBN: Print 978-1-64611-687-4 | Ebook 978-1-64611-688-1

R0